The Barbecue Cookbook

The Best Recipes and Techniques to
Become the King of Barbecue

by

David S. Seymour

TABLE OF CONTENTS

TABLE OF CONTENTS

TABLE OF CONTENTS

BBQ Chicken Pizza I

3 boneless chicken breast halves, cooked and cubed

1 cup hickory flavored barbeque sauce | 1 tablespoon honey

1 teaspoon molasses | 1/3 cup brown sugar

1/2 bunch fresh cilantro, chopped | 1 (12 inch) pre-baked pizza crust

1 cup smoked Gouda cheese, shredded | 1 cup thinly sliced red onion

Directions:

Preheat oven to 425 degrees F (220 degrees C).
In a saucepan over medium high heat, combine chicken, barbeque sauce,
honey, molasses, brown sugar and cilantro. Bring to a boil.

Spread chicken mixture evenly over pizza crust, and top with cheese
and onions. Bake for 15 to 20 minutes, or until cheese is melted.

2

Sweet and Tangy BBQ Sauce

Ingredients:

2 tablespoons butter

1 small onion, minced

2 cups ketchup | 1/2 cup cider vinegar

1/4 cup water | 1/4 cup apple juice

1/4 cup Worcestershire sauce

2 tablespoons brown sugar

2 tablespoons molasses

2 tablespoons honey

2 teaspoons dry mustard powder

1 teaspoon chili powder

1 teaspoon garlic powder

1 teaspoon ground cayenne pepper

Directions:

Melt the butter in saucepan over medium heat. Stir in the onion,
and cook until tender. Mix in ketchup, cider vinegar, water, apple juice,
Worcestershire sauce, brown sugar, molasses, honey, mustard powder,
chili powder, garlic powder, and cayenne pepper.
Bring to a boil. Reduce heat to low, and simmer 30 minutes,
stirring occasionally.

4

Elaine's Sweet and Tangy Loose Beef BBQ

Ingredients:

7 pounds boneless chuck roast | 1 cup water

3 tablespoons white vinegar | 4 tablespoons brown sugar

2 teaspoons dry mustard | 4 tablespoons Worcestershire sauce

3 cups ketchup | 2 teaspoons salt

3/4 teaspoon ground black pepper

1/4 teaspoon cayenne pepper | 6 cloves garlic, minced

Directions:

Place the roast into a slow cooker along with the water.
Cover, and cook on LOW for 2 to 4 hours, or until beef can be easily
shredded with a fork.

Shred the beef, removing fat as you go.
Remove 1/2 cup of the broth from the slow cooker, and reserve for later.
Add the vinegar, brown sugar, dry mustard, Worcestershire sauce
and ketchup. Mix in the salt, pepper, cayenne, and garlic.
Stir so that the meat is well coated.

Cover, and continue to cook beef on LOW for an additional 4 to 6 hours.
Add the reserved broth only if necessary to maintain moisture.
Serve on toasted buns. The meat can be frozen for future use.

5

6

Christian's Killer BBQ and Grill Marinade

Ingredients:

2/3 cup light olive oil | 1/3 cup apple cider vinegar

1/4 cup Worcestershire sauce 1/4 cup soy sauce

1/4 cup honey | 1/4 cup molasses

1/4 cup whiskey | 1/3 cup seasoning salt

1/3 cup salt-free seasoning blend 1/4 cup garlic powder

1 tablespoon ginger | 2 tablespoons browning sauce

2 tablespoons prepared mustard

1 tablespoon hickory-flavored liquid smoke

Directions:

Place oil, vinegar, Worcestershire sauce, soy sauce, honey, molasses, whiskey, seasoning salt, salt-free seasoning blend, garlic powder, ginger, browning sauce, mustard, and liquid smoke in a resealable container or bottle, and shake well.
Store marinade in refrigerator until ready to use.

Bring marinade to room temperature and shake well before each use.

Oven BBQ

1 pound hardwood chips

1 1/2 cups ketchup | 1/2 cup brown sugar

1 (12 fluid ounce) can or bottle beer

1/4 cup distilled white vinegar | 1/2 cup red wine

1/2 medium onion, diced | 1 cup diced green bell pepper

1 tablespoon black pepper

1 (4 pound) whole chicken, cut into 4 pieces

Directions:

Place wood chips in warm water, and soak for 2 to 3 hours.

Preheat oven to 350 degrees F (175 degrees C).

In a small saucepan, blend the ketchup, brown sugar, beer, vinegar, and wine.

Mix in the onion, bell pepper, and black pepper. Simmer until thickened, approximately 10 minutes.

Spread wet wood chips evenly in the bottom of a broiler pan, adding enough water to ensure chips remain moist while cooking. Cover with broiler pan grate, and arrange chicken pieces on top. Coat chicken with the sauce, and cook approximately 1 hour, basting regularly.

In a small saucepan over medium heat, simmer any remaining sauce to be used additionally for dipping when served.

Ryan's Gourmet BBQ Sauce

1 cup tomato sauce | 1/4 cup honey | 1/4 cup soy sauce

6 tablespoons distilled white vinegar

1/4 cup light corn syrup | 3 tablespoons Worcestershire sauce

2 tablespoons hoisin sauce | 1/2 teaspoon cayenne pepper

|salt and freshly ground black pepper to taste

Directions:

In a saucepan over medium heat, mix the tomato sauce, honey, soy sauce, vinegar, corn syrup, Worcestershire sauce, hoisin sauce, cayenne pepper, salt, and pepper. Cook 30 minutes, until thickened. Cool, and use immediately.

Honey Mustard BBQ Pork Chops

Ingredients:

1/3 cup honey

3 tablespoons orange juice

1 tablespoon apple cider vinegar

1 teaspoon white wine

1 teaspoon Worcestershire sauce

2 teaspoons onion powder, or to taste

1/4 teaspoon dried tarragon

3 tablespoons Dijon mustard

8 thin cut pork chops

Directions:

Place honey, orange juice, vinegar, wine, Worcestershire sauce, onion powder, tarragon, and mustard in a large resealable plastic bag. Slash fatty edge of each chop in about three places without cutting into the meat; this will prevent the meat from curling during cooking. Place chops in the plastic bag, and marinate in the refrigerator for at least 2 hours.

Preheat grill for high heat.

Lightly oil grill grate. Place chops on grill, and discard marinade. Cook chops for 6 to 8 minutes, turning once, or to desired doneness.

14

Grilled Picante BBQ Chicken

Ingredients:

3/4 cup Pace® Picante Sauce | 1/4 cup barbecue sauce
6 skinless, boneless chicken breast halves

Directions:

Stir the picante sauce and barbecue sauce in a small bowl.
Reserve all but 1/2 cup picante sauce mixture to serve with the chicken.

Lightly oil the grill rack and heat the grill to medium. Grill the chicken for
15 minutes or until cooked through,
turning and brushing often with the remaining picante sauce mixture.
Discard the remaining picante sauce mixture.

Serve the chicken with the reserved picante sauce mixture.

Honey Garlic BBQ Sauce II

Ingredients:

2 cups ketchup | 1 bulb garlic, peeled and crushed

1 cup water | 2 tablespoons hot sauce | 1/4 cup honey

2 tablespoons molasses | 2 tablespoons brown sugar

1 teaspoon Worcestershire sauce

1 teaspoon soy sauce | 1 teaspoon salt

2 tablespoons Cajun seasonin | 1/2 cup butter

1 pinch paprika | 1 pinch crushed red pepper

1 pinch ground white pepper | 1 pinch ground black pepper

2 tablespoons cornstarch | 1 tablespoon water

Directions:

In a large saucepan over medium low heat, mix together ketchup, garlic, 1 cup of water, hot sauce, honey, molasses, brown sugar, Worcestershire sauce, soy sauce, salt, Cajun seasoning, paprika, red pepper, white pepper and black pepper. Allow the mixture to simmer approximately 30 minutes.

In a small bowl, dissolve cornstarch in 1 tablespoon of water. Adjust amount of water as needed to fully dissolve cornstarch.
Stir into the sauce mixture. Continue simmering approximately 15 minutes.

Stir butter into the sauce mixture. Continue simmering mixture approximately 15 more minutes, or until butter is melted and the sauce has begun to thicken. Serve over meats prepared as desired.

Simple BBQ Sauce

/2 (1 ounce) package dry onion soup mix
1/2 cup packed brown sugar 2 cups ketchup
1 teaspoon Worcestershire sauce

Directions:

In a medium bowl, mix together onion soup mix, sugar, ketchup,
and Worcestershire sauce. Do not use until the last few minutes
of cooking, because this sweet sauce
will burn if cooked for too long or over too high heat.

Kalbi (Korean BBQ Short Ribs)

Ingredients:

2 cups ketchup

1/2 cup water

1/2 cup white vinegar

1/2 cup honey

2 tablespoons Worcestershire sauce

1 tablespoon dried minced onion

1/4 teaspoon pepper

1 dash garlic powder dash cayenne pepper

2 1/2 pounds frozen fully cooked meatballs

Directions:

In a bowl, stir together the soy sauce, brown sugar, water, garlic, green onions, and sesame oil until the sugar has dissolved.

Place the ribs in a large plastic zipper bag. Pour the marinade over the ribs, squeeze out all the air, and refrigerate the bag for 3 hours to overnight.

Preheat an outdoor grill for medium-high heat, and lightly oil the grate. Remove the ribs from the bag, shake off the excess marinade, and discard the marinade. Grill the ribs on the preheated grill until the meat is still pink but not bloody nearest the bone, 5 to 7 minutes per side.

Korean BBQ Short Ribs (Gal-Bi)

3/4 cup soy sauce

3/4 cup water

3 tablespoons white vinegar

1/4 cup dark brown sugar

2 tablespoons white sugar

1 tablespoon black pepper

2 tablespoons sesame oil

1/4 cup minced garlic

1/2 large onion, minced

3 pounds Korean-style short ribs (beef chuck flanken, cut 1/3 to 1/2 inch thick across bones)

Directions:

Pour soy sauce, water, and vinegar into a large, non-metallic bowl. Whisk in brown sugar, white sugar, pepper, sesame oil, garlic, and onion until the sugars have dissolved. Submerge the ribs in this marinade, and cover with plastic wrap. Refrigerate 7 to 12 hours; the longer, the better.

Preheat an outdoor grill for medium-high heat.

Remove ribs from the marinade, shake off excess, and discard the marinade. Cook on preheated grill until the meat is no longer pink, 5 to 7 minutes per side.

BBQ Potato Roast

Ingredients:

10 potatoes, peeled and halved | 1/2 cup vegetable oil
2 tablespoons seasoned salt

Directions:

Preheat grill for high heat.

Place potatoes in a large saucepan with enough lightly salted water to cover.
Bring to a boil. Cook 15 minutes, or until tender but firm.

Drain potatoes, and pat dry. Coat thoroughly with vegetable oil
and seasoned salt.

Place potatoes on the preheated grill. Cook approximately 20 minutes,
turning periodically.

Sweet 'n' Spicy BBQ Sauce

Ingredients:

2 cups packed brown sugar | 2 cups ketchup
1 cup water | 1 cup cider vinegar | 1 cup finely chopped onion
1 (8 ounce) can tomato sauce | 1 cup corn syrup | 1 cup molasses
1 (6 ounce) can tomato paste | 2 tablespoons Worcestershire sauce
1 tablespoon garlic pepper blend
1 tablespoon liquid smoke flavoring (optional)
1 tablespoon prepared mustard | 1 teaspoon onion salt
1 teaspoon celery salt

Directions:

In a large saucepan, combine all ingredients. Bring to a boil. Reduce heat; simmer, uncovered, for 15 minutes or until the flavors are blended. Remove from the heat; cool.

BBQ Sauce for Chicken

Ingredients:

3 tablespoons
vegetable oil

2 onions, chopped

5 cloves garlic, minced

1 (12 fluid ounce) can
frozen orange juice
concentrate, thawed

2 teaspoons
mustard powder

2 cups ketchup

1 lemon, juiced

1/2 cup Burgundy wine

salt and pepper to taste

Directions:

In a medium skillet saute onion and garlic for 4 to 5 minutes
(until translucent). Add the orange juice, mustard, ketchup, lemon,
Chianti/burgundy, salt and pepper. Simmer all together over low heat for
30 minutes, then put through food processor.
Sauce may be thinned with water to taste, if desired.

BBQ Chicken

Ingredients:

3 tablespoons vegetable oil | 1 1/2 cups cider vinegar
1 tablespoon salt | 1/4 teaspoon ground black pepper
2 teaspoons poultry seasoning | 2 pounds cut up chicken pieces

Directions:

Heat grill to medium heat.

In a small skillet combine the oil, vinegar, salt and pepper and put over low heat. Add the poultry seasoning while stirring constantly; when sauce mixes well and starts to bubble, it is done.

Place chicken on hot grill and brush with sauce. Grill for 45 to 60 minutes, turning every 5 to 10 minutes, and brush chicken with sauce after each turning. Grill until chicken is done and juices run clear.
(Note: Be sure to keep an eye on the chicken as it cooks, as it tends to have flair ups due to the oil and chicken drippings!)

Smokin' Jack BBQ Sauce

Ingredients:

8 cups ketchup

6 ounces chipotle peppers in adobo sauce

1/2 cup apple cider vinegar

1/2 cup molasses

1 1/2 teaspoons onion powder

1 1/2 teaspoons garlic powder

1 1/2 teaspoons ground mustard

1 1/2 teaspoons smoked paprika

1 1/2 teaspoons ground coriander

1 tablespoon kosher salt

1 1/2 teaspoons freshly cracked black pepper

1 cup dark brown sugar

1 cup whiskey (such as Jack Daniels®)

2 tablespoons liquid hickory smoke flavoring

Directions:

Combine the ketchup, chipotle peppers in their sauce, apple cider vinegar, molasses, onion powder, garlic powder, ground mustard, smoked paprika, coriander, salt, black pepper, brown sugar, whiskey, and liquid smoke flavoring in a large pot, and bring to a gentle boil over medium heat, stirring frequently. Cook the sauce for 15 minutes, then reduce heat to low and simmer 15 more minutes, stirring often. Use immediately or refrigerate.

Firehouse BBQ Sauce

Ingredients:

1 (46 fluid ounce) bottle ketchup | 1 1/2 cups apple cider vinegar

2 cups packed brown sugar | 1/2 cup butter, cut into pieces

2 tablespoons red pepper flakes, or to taste

Directions:

Pour ketchup into a large saucepan. Pour vinegar into the ketchup bottle,
shake to loosen any remaining ketchup, and pour into the saucepan.
Save the bottle, and clean. Stir in the brown sugar, butter,
and red pepper flakes. Cook over medium heat until almost boiling,
but do not boil. For convenience, refrigerate leftover sauce in the
clean ketchup bottle.

BBQ Feta and Hot Banana Pepper Turkey Burgers

Ingredients:

1 pound ground turkey | 1/4 cup seeded, chopped banana peppers
1/2 cup crumbled feta cheese | salt and pepper to taste

Directions:

Preheat an outdoor grill for high heat.

In a bowl, mix the turkey, peppers, and feta cheese.
Season with salt and pepper. Form the mixture into 4 patties.

Cook patties about 8 minutes per side on the prepared grill,
to an internal temperature of 180 degrees F (85 degrees C).

Root Beer BBQ Sauce

Ingredients:

2 cups root beer | 2 cups ketchup
1/2 cup no-pulp orange juice | 1/4 cup Worcestershire sauce
1/4 cup molasses | 1 teaspoon ground ginger
1 teaspoon hot paprika | 1 teaspoon chipotle chile powder
2 teaspoons garlic powder | 2 teaspoons onion powder
1/2 teaspoon crushed red pepper flakes

Directions:

Stir together the root beer, ketchup, orange juice, Worcestershire sauce, and molasses in a saucepan. Season with ginger, paprika, chipotle powder, garlic powder, onion powder, and red pepper flakes. Bring to a boil over high heat, then reduce heat to medium-low and simmer 15 minutes, stirring occasionally. Use immediately or store in the refrigerator up to a week.

BBQ Peanut Butter Chicken

1 cup SMUCKER'S® Natural Peanut Butter

1/4 cup soy sauce

1/4 cup white wine vinegar

1/4 cup lemon juice

6 cloves garlic, chopped

1 teaspoon red pepper flakes

2 teaspoons ginger, finely chopped

2 1/2 pounds chicken breasts, boneless and skinless,
cut into 1 1/2-inch strips.

Directions:

Prepare marinade 2 hours before ready to grill.

Mix the ingredients, except the chicken in a blender until combined.

If too thick, add up to a cup of water to thin.

Marinate the chicken for approximately 2 hours.

Lightly oil the medium/hot BBQ grill.

Place chicken on the grill for 6-8 minutes.

Australian BBQ Meatballs

Ingredients:

1 pound ground beef | 1/2 cup bread crumbs

2 small onions, chopped | 1 tablespoon curry powder

1 tablespoon dried Italian seasoning | 1 egg, beaten

1 clove garlic, minced | 1/2 cup milk

1/2 teaspoon salt | 1/2 teaspoon ground black pepper

1 tablespoon margarine | 2 small onions, chopped

3/4 cup ketchup | 1/2 cup beef stock | 1/4 cup steak sauce

1/2 cup Worcestershire sauce | 2 tablespoons white vinegar

2 tablespoons instant coffee granules

1/2 cup packed brown sugar 3 tablespoons lemon juice

Directions:

Preheat the oven to 375 degrees F (190 degrees C). In a medium bowl, mix together the ground beef, bread crumbs, 2 onions, curry powder, Italian seasoning, egg, garlic, salt and pepper. Gradually mix in the milk until you have a nice texture for forming meatballs. You may not need all of the milk. Form the meat into balls slightly smaller than golf balls. Place them in a greased baking dish. Bake the meatballs for 30 minutes in the preheated oven. Once the meatballs are in the oven, start making the sauce straight away.

Melt the margarine in a saucepan over medium heat. Add the remaining onions, and cook until browned. Stir in the ketchup, beef stock, steak sauce, Worcestershire sauce, vinegar, instant coffee, brown sugar and lemon juice. Bring to a boil over medium heat, and simmer, stirring occasionally, until the meatballs are done.

Remove the meatballs from the oven, and drain any excess grease. Pour the sauce over them, and return to the oven. Bake for an additional 30 minutes.

These meatballs taste even better after they have been left to rest for a while to soak up the sauce. I usually make the recipe at lunchtime and let it cool. I put it back in the oven at about 200 degrees for 43 approximately 15 minutes to reheat for dinner. This is not necessary but it makes it taste even better!

Extra Simple BBQ Banana

Ingredients:

2 bananas | 4 scoops vanilla ice cream

1 teaspoon chopped fresh mint (optional)

Directions:

Place whole, unpeeled bananas on grill, turning occasionally until the peel is blackened. Remove stems and skin.

Slice bananas, and serve over vanilla ice cream with mint garnish

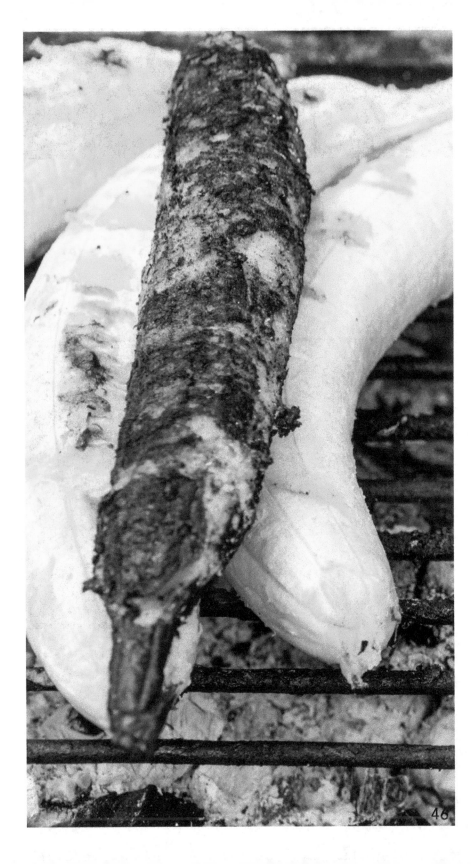

Tickety-Tock BBQ Sauce

Ingredients:

1 (12 ounce) bottle barbeque sauce

1/2 cup apple cider vinegar | 1/4 cup ketchup

2 tablespoons stone ground horseradish mustard

Directions:

In a saucepan, combine the barbeque sauce, cider vinegar, ketchup, and horseradish mustard. Bring to a boil and cook for 1 minute. Use with your favorite barbequed meat.

48

BBQ Potatoes with Green Onions

Ingredients:

6 large potatoes, peeled | 4 green onions, finely chopped
2 tablespoons butter | salt and ground black pepper to taste

Directions:

Preheat an outdoor grill for high heat.

Microwave potatoes on High 5 to 8 minutes, until tender but still firm.
Cool slightly, and cube.

Place cubed potatoes on a large piece of foil. Top with green onions.
Dot with butter, and season with salt and pepper.
Tightly seal foil around the potatoes.

Cook on the prepared grill 20 to 30 minutes, until tender.

Wildfire BBQ Beef on Buns

3 pounds chuck roast or round steak | 1 small onion, thinly sliced

1 cup Bob Evans® Wildfire BBQ Sauce | 12 rolls or buns

1/2 cup apricot preserves | 2 tablespoons Dijon mustard

Directions:

Place beef and onion into slow cooker. Combine Wildfire sauce, preserves
and mustard and pour into slow cooker. Cover and heat on low
for 8 to 10 hours or until meat is tender. Remove meat and shred with 2 forks.
Combine shredded meat with sauce and serve on buns.

Hot and Spicy BBQ Sauce

Ingredients:

1 (46 fluid ounce) bottle ketchup | 2 cups apple cider vinegar

1 cup SPLENDA® No Calorie Sweetener, Granulated | 1/2 cup butter

1 tablespoon red pepper flakes | 1/4 cup Texas style hot sauce

Directions:

In a large saucepan or soup pot, stir together the ketchup, cider vinegar, SPLENDA® Granulated Sweetener, butter, red pepper flakes and hot sauce. Cook over medium heat until the butter is melted and the sauce is heated through

BBQ BeerBrat Kabobs

Ingredients:

1 (19 ounce) package Bob
EvansB® Beer Bratwurst, cut into 1-inch pieces
1 green bell pepper, cut into 1-inch pieces
1 medium zucchini, cut into 1-inch pieces
1 red bell pepper, cut into 1-inch pieces
1 medium yellow squash, cut into | 1-inch pieces
2 cups fresh button mushroom caps
1 medium red onion, cut into 1-inch pieces
2 cups Bob EvansB® Wildfire BBQ Sauce | 6 (10 inch) wooden skewers

Directions:

Soak wooden skewers in water 30 minutes. Alternately thread bratwurst
and vegetables onto skewers. Grill or broil kabobs 12 to 15 minutes
or until brats are cooked through, turning and brushing occasionally
with barbecue sauce. Refrigerate leftovers.

Adult Watermelon for BBQ's

Ingredients:

1 seedless watermelon | 1 1/2 cups rum, or as needed

Directions:

Rinse the outer rind of the watermelon thoroughly, and pat dry.
Set the watermelon in a position so it will not roll over. Press the tip of a
funnel through the rind of the melon. If using a plastic funnel,
you may need to cut a hole.

Situate the melon on a towel in the bottom of the refrigerator or
on the counter. Pour rum into the funnel a little at a time, refilling as it seeps
into the melon. I start the afternoon before, since we usually leave to go
to events in the morning. Allow the melon to marinate at least a few hours,
before removing the funnel. Slice just before serving.

Slow Cooker Carolina BBQ

Ingredients:

1 (5 pound) bone-in pork shoulder roast

1 tablespoon salt ground black pepper

1 1/2 cups apple cider vinegar

2 tablespoons brown sugar

1 1/2 tablespoons hot pepper sauce

2 teaspoons cayenne pepper

2 teaspoons crushed red pepper flakes

Directions:

Place the pork shoulder into a slow cooker and season with salt and pepper.
Pour the vinegar around the pork. Cover, and cook on Low for 12 hours.
Pork should easily pull apart into strands.

Remove the pork from the slow cooker and discard any bones.
Strain out the liquid, and save 2 cups.
Discard any extra. Shred the pork using tongs or two forks,
and return to the slow cooker.
Stir the brown sugar, hot pepper sauce, cayenne pepper,
and red pepper flakes into the reserved sauce.
Mix into the pork in the slow cooker.
Cover and keep on Low setting until serving.

60

Eastern North Carolina BBQ Sauce

Ingredients:

1 cup white vinegar | 1 cup cider vinegar
1 tablespoon brown sugar | 1 tablespoon cayenne pepper
1 tablespoon hot pepper sauce (e. g. Tabascoв„ў), or to taste
1 teaspoon salt | 1 teaspoon ground black pepper

Directions:

Combine the white vinegar, cider vinegar, brown sugar, cayenne pepper, h
ot pepper sauce, salt and pepper in a jar or bottle with a tight-fitting lid.
Refrigerate for 1 to 2 days before using so that the flavors will blend.
Shake occasionally, and store for up to 2 months in the refrigerator.

Apple and BBQ Sauce Baby Back Ribs

Ingredients:

4 cups barbeque sauce | 4 cups applesauce
4 pounds baby back pork ribs | salt and black pepper to taste
cayenne pepper to taste | garlic powder to taste

Directions:

Mix the barbeque sauce and applesauce in bowl. Place ribs on a large sheet of heavy duty aluminum foil, and rub on all sides with the salt, pepper, cayenne pepper, and garlic powder. Pour sauce over ribs to coat.
Seal ribs in the foil. Marinate in the refrigerator 8 hours, or overnight.

Preheat grill for high heat.

Place ribs in foil on the grill grate, and cook 1 hour.
Remove ribs from foil, and place directly on the grill grate.
Continue cooking 30 minutes, basting frequently with the sauce,
until ribs are done.

64

Grilled Spice Rubbed Chicken Breasts

1 cup Hellmann's® or Best Foods® Real Mayonnaise

2 tablespoons cider vinegar

2 tablespoons horseradish

1/8 teaspoon cayenne chili powder

4 (6 ounce) boneless, skinless chicken breast

2 tablespoons canola oil

2 tablespoons Bobby Flay's Sixteen Spice Rub for Poultry or your favorite spice rub or grill seasoning

Directions:

Combine Hellmann's® or Best Foods® Real Mayonnaise, vinegar, horseradish and chili powder in small bowl. Season, if desired, with salt and pepper; reserve 1/2 cup sauce and set aside.

Brush chicken on both sides with oil and season, if desired, with salt and pepper. Evenly sprinkle top of chicken with spice rub.

Grill chicken, rub-side down, until golden brown and crust has formed, about 4 minutes. Brush chicken with mayonnaise mixture, turn over and cook an additional 4 minutes or until chicken is thoroughly cooked. Remove to serving platter, then cover loosely with aluminum foil and let sit 5 minutes before serving. Slice each breast and serve with reserved 1/2 cup sauce on the side.

66

Nonie's Best BBQ

1 (14 ounce) bottle ketchup | 1/2 cup water

1/4 cup white sugar | 1 tablespoon brown sugar

1 tablespoon red wine vinegar

1 tablespoon prepared yellow mustard

1 teaspoon salt | 1/4 teaspoon ground black pepper

1/4 teaspoon paprika | 2 pounds ground beef

2 teaspoons minced onion | 12 hamburger buns, split

Directions:

Whisk together the ketchup, water, white sugar, brown sugar, vinegar,
mustard, salt, pepper, and paprika in a large saucepan.
Bring to a simmer over medium-high heat; reduce heat to medium-low
and simmer 15 minutes.

Meanwhile, heat a large skillet over medium-high heat; cook and stir the
ground beef and onion in the hot skillet until the beef is crumbly,
evenly browned, and no longer pink; drain and discard any excess grease.
Stir the beef into the simmering barbeque sauce.
Simmer together for 10 minutes. Spoon into the buns to serve.

BBQ Glazed Homemade Meatballs

Ingredients:

1 1/2 pounds ground beef | 1 egg, lightly beaten

1 cup quick cooking oats | 6 1/2 ounces evaporated milk

1 teaspoon salt | 1/4 teaspoon pepper

1/2 teaspoon garlic powder | 1 tablespoon chili powder

1/2 cup chopped onion | 1 cup ketchup

1/4 teaspoon minced garlic | 1 cup brown sugar

1/4 cup chopped onion | 1 tablespoon liquid smoke flavoring

Directions:

Preheat oven to 350 degrees F (175 degrees C).
Lightly grease a medium baking dish.

In a bowl, mix beef, egg, oats, evaporated milk, salt, pepper, garlic powder, chili powder, and 1/2 cup onion. Form into 1 1/2 inch balls and arrange in a single layer in the baking dish.

In a separate bowl, mix ketchup, garlic, sugar, 1/4 cup onion, a nd liquid smoke. Pour evenly over the meatballs.

Bake uncovered 1 hour in the preheated oven, until the minimum internal temperature of a meatball reaches 160 degrees F (72 degrees C).

69

BBQ Meatballs

Ingredients:

4 eggs, beaten | 1/2 cup vodka

1/2 cup water | 1 tablespoon Worcestershire sauce

2 tablespoons dried minced onion flakes

1 teaspoon garlic powder, or to taste

1/2 teaspoon salt, or to taste

1/2 teaspoon ground black pepper, or to taste

3 pounds ground beef | 2 pounds ground turkey

1 (15 ounce) package Italian seasoned bread crumbs

2 (28 ounce) cans crushed tomatoes

2 (14.25 ounce) cans tomato puree

1 (18 ounce) bottle hickory smoke flavored barbeque sauce

1 (8 ounce) can crushed pineapple | 1 cup brown sugar

1 (14 ounce) bottle ketchup | 1/2 cup vodka

2 tablespoons dried minced onion flakes

1 teaspoon garlic powder, or to taste

1/2 teaspoon salt, or to taste

1/2 teaspoon ground black pepper, or to taste

Directions:

In a large bowl, combine eggs, 1/2 cup vodka and Worcestershire sauce.
Season with 2 tablespoons onion flakes, garlic powder, salt and pepper.
Mix in ground beef, ground turkey and bread crumbs.
Shape into meatballs, and set aside.

In a very large pot over medium heat, Combine crushed tomatoes,
tomato puree, barbeque sauce, pineapple, brown sugar, ketchup,
and 1/2 cup vodka. Season to taste with onion flakes, garlic powder,
salt and pepper. Bring to a boil, reduce heat and let simmer.

Heat a large heavy skillet over medium heat.
Cook meatballs until evenly brown on all sides. Carefully place into sauce,
and simmer for at least an hour.

Vinegar Based BBQ Sauce

Ingredients:

1 cup cider vinegar | 1 tablespoon salt

1/2 teaspoon cayenne pepper | 1 tablespoon brown sugar

1 teaspoon crushed red pepper flakes

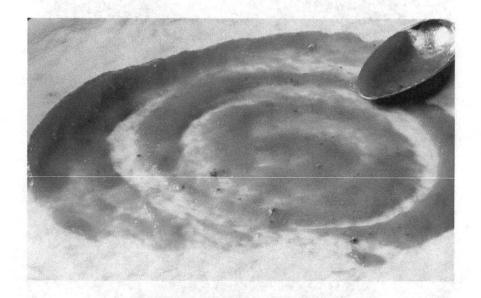

Directions:

In a small bowl, combine the vinegar, salt, cayenne pepper,
crushed red pepper flakes and brown sugar.
Mix well and allow ingredients to mesh for about
4 to 8 hours before using

Caribbean BBQ Sauce II

2 tablespoons olive oil | 1 cup minced onion

2 cloves garlic, minced | 2 cups ketchup

3 (1 inch) pieces fresh ginger root, minced

1/2 cup brown sugar | 1/4 cup molasses

1/2 cup spiced rum, divided 3 tablespoons hoisin sauce

2 tablespoons tomato paste | 2 tablespoons sherry vinegar

1 tablespoon chili powder | 1/8 teaspoon cayenne pepper

Directions:

Heat the olive oil in a saucepan over medium-high heat.
Stir in the onion, garlic, and ginger, and cook until tender.
Reduce heat to low. Mix in ketchup, brown sugar, molasses, rum,
hoisin sauce, tomato paste, vinegar, chili powder, and cayenne pepper.
Cook and stir 5 minutes, until well blended and heated through.
Stir in remaining rum.

BBQ Turkey

2 cups butter, divided

1 (15 pound) whole turkey, neck and giblets removed

1/4 cup chicken soup base | 3 sweet onions, peeled and cut into wedges

5 apples, cored and cut into wedges

2 tablespoons minced garlic, or to taste

1 (750 milliliter) bottle dry white wine

Directions:

Preheat a gas grill for low heat.

Rub some of the butter all over the turkey, inside and out,
then rub all over with chicken base. Cut remaining butter into cubes and
toss with onions, apples, and garlic in a large bowl.
Stuff the bird with this mixture and place in a disposable aluminum
roasting pan. Fold the turkey skin around the neck area to cover
the hole and then turn the turkey over and pour wine into the opening
at the other end until the turkey is full or the bottle is empty.
Set the turkey breast side up.

Place the roasting pan on the grill and cover loosely with aluminum foil.
If you have a pop up timer or heat safe meat thermometer,
insert it into the turkey breast. Close the lid.

Roast until the temperature in the breast reads 170 degrees F (75 degrees C)
and the temperature in the thickest part of the thigh reads
180 degrees C (80 degrees C), /about 4 hours depending on the
temperature of your grill. When the temperature is getting close, remove
the aluminum foil covering the turkey and allow it to brown
during the final minutes of cooking. If it starts to brown too much, just cover
it back up. Allow the turkey to rest for at least 20 minutes before carving.

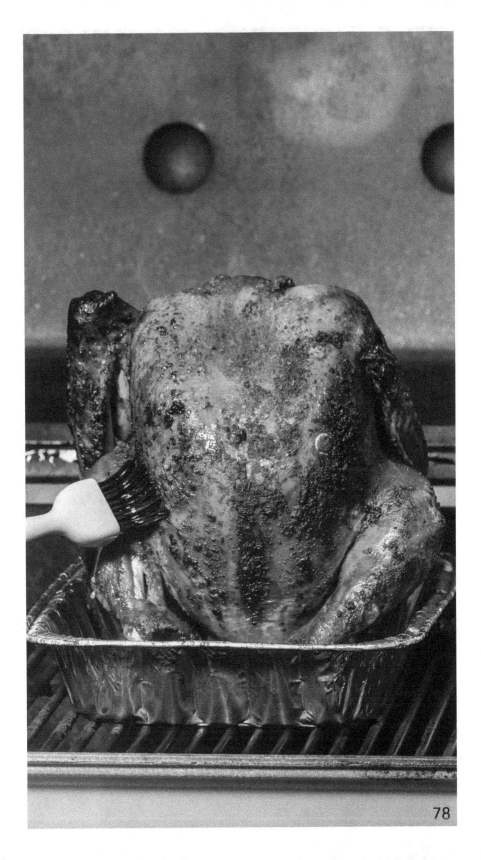

Bourbon Whiskey BBQ Sauce

Ingredients:

1/2 onion, minced

4 cloves garlic, minced

3/4 cup bourbon whiskey

1/2 teaspoon ground black pepper

1/2 tablespoon salt

2 cups ketchup

1/4 cup tomato paste

1/3 cup cider vinegar

2 tablespoons liquid smoke flavoring

1/4 cup Worcestershire sauce

1/2 cup packed brown sugar

1/3 teaspoon hot pepper sauce, or to taste

Directions:

In a large skillet over medium heat, combine the onion, garlic, and whiskey.
Simmer for 10 minutes, or until onion is translucent.
Mix in the ground black pepper, salt, ketchup, tomato paste, vinegar,
liquid smoke, Worcestershire sauce, brown sugar, and hot pepper sauce.

Bring to a boil. Reduce heat to medium-low, and simmer for 20 minutes.
Run sauce through a strainer if you prefer a smooth sauce.

BBQ Chicken and Bacon Bread

Ingredients:

1 egg | 1/4 cup water

3 cooked skinless, boneless chicken breast halves, chopped

6 slices bacon - cooked and crumbled

1 small green bell pepper, chopped

1 1/2 cups honey barbecue sauce, divided

1 (8 ounce) package shredded

Cheddar-Monterey Jack cheese, blend, divided

all-purpose flour for rolling

1 (11.5 ounce) can refrigerated crusty French loaf dough

Directions:

Preheat an oven to 350 degrees F (175 degrees C).
Whisk egg and water; set aside.

Combine chicken, bacon, bell pepper, 1 cup barbecue sauce, and 1 cup of
shredded cheese blend. The barbecue sauce should coat the meat;
if the mixture is too dry, add more sauce.

Unroll dough on smooth, clean, well-floured surface,
and spread or roll out to 1/4 inch thick, keeping rectangular shape.
Spread the chicken mixture down the middle of the dough.
Top the mixture with more barbecue sauce and the rest of the cheese.
Fold one side of dough over mixture. Brush egg wash on edge of
folded dough; then fold over other side of dough, sealing with egg wash.
Seal both ends of loaf well with egg wash and brush it over the
top of the bread

Carefully place the bread on a greased baking sheet.
Bake in the preheated oven until golden brown,
about 25 to 35 minutes. Cool slightly before slicing.

Uncle Earl's NC BBQ Sauce

Ingredients:

1 (46 fluid ounce) bottle ketchup | 1/2 cup butter

2 cups apple cider vinegar | 1 cup white sugar

1 tablespoon red pepper flakes | 1/4 cup Texas style hot sauce

Directions:

In a large saucepan or soup pot, stir together the
ketchup, cider vinegar, sugar, butter, red pepper flakes and hot sauce.
Cook over medium heat until the butter is melted and the sauce is heated
through. Use right away, or store in the refrigerator for up to a month.

Owen's BBQ Chicken

Ingredients:

2 tablespoons vegetable oil | 1 onion, finely chopped

2 cloves crushed garlic | 3/4 cup ketchup

2 tablespoons Worcestershire sauce

2 tablespoons white wine vinegar

2 tablespoons brown sugar | 1/2 cup water

salt and pepper to taste 10 chicken legs

Directions:

Heat oil in a medium saucepan over medium heat. Add the onion and
garlic and saute for 5 to 10 minutes, or until onion is tender.
Then add the ketchup, Worcestershire sauce, vinegar, brown sugar
and water. Mix together well and season with salt and pepper to taste.
Reduce heat to low, cover and simmer for 20 minutes.
Set aside, covered, and let cool.

Place chicken in a shallow, nonporous dish and pour sauce over chicken,
reserving some sauce in a separate container for basting.
Cover chicken and marinate in the refrigerator for at least one hour,
or overnight. Cover reserved sauce, if any, and keep in the refrigerator.

Preheat an outdoor grill for medium high heat and lightly oil grate.

Grill chicken over medium high heat for 8 to 12 minutes per side,
basting occasionally with the sauce,if any, until internal temperature reaches
180 degrees F (80 degrees C).

BBQ Eggs

Ingredients:

4 eggs

2 1/2 tablespoons barbecue sauce

2 tablespoons milk

1 1/2 teaspoons dried dill

1 1/2 teaspoons mustard powder

1 1/2 teaspoons minced garlic

1 tablespoon butter or margarine

1/2 cup shredded Cheddar cheese

Directions:

In a medium bowl, whisk together the eggs, barbeque sauce, milk, dill, mustard powder and garlic.

Melt butter or margarine in a large skillet over medium heat. Pour in the egg mixture, and cook stirring frequently until eggs are scrambled and cooked through. Remove from heat, and sprinkle cheese over the top. Let stand for a minute to melt cheese, then serve immediately.

BBQ Dry Rub

Ingredients:

1 1/4 cups white sugar

1 1/4 cups brown sugar

1/2 cup salt

1/4 cup freshly ground black pepper

1/4 cup paprika

Directions:

In a medium bowl, mix together white and brown sugars, salt, pepper, and paprika. Rub onto pork 10 minutes prior to grilling.
Store any leftover rub in a sealed container.

Cranberry BBQ Chicken

Ingredients:

1 (2 to 3 pound) whole chicken, cut into pieces

2 tablespoons butter

1/2 teaspoon salt

1/4 teaspoon ground black pepper

1/2 cup chopped celery 1 onion, chopped

1 (16 ounce) can whole cranberry sauce

1 cup barbecue sauce

Directions:

Preheat oven to 350 degrees F (175 degrees C).

In a large skillet brown the chicken in butter/margarine.
Season with salt and pepper. Remove from skillet and place in a
lightly greased 9x13 inch baking dish.

In the drippings (in the skillet), saute onion and celery until tender.

Add cranberry sauce and barbecue sauce. Mix well.

Pour cranberry mixture over chicken and bake in the preheated
oven for 90 minutes, basting every 15 minutes.

91

BBQ Hotdogs on Rice

1 cup uncooked long grain white rice | 2 cups water

1 pound kielbasa sausage, thinly slice | 1/2 cup dark molasses

2 tablespoons distilled white vinegar | 1 (10 ounce) can tomato sauce

1/4 cup barbeque sauce (optional)

Directions:

Place the rice and water in a pot, and bring to a boil.
Reduce heat to low, cover, and simmer 20 minutes.

Cook the kielbasa in a skillet over medium heat until evenly browned.
Mix in the molasses, vinegar, tomato sauce, and barbeque sauce.
Continue to cook until heated through. Serve over the rice.

Southern BBQ Sauce

Ingredients:

1 1/4 gallons apple cider vinegar

1 (28 ounce) bottle ketchup

5 1/2 ounces chili pepper flakes

4 ounces cayenne pepper

2 ounces ground black pepper

3 ounces ground paprika

Directions:

In a large, clean tub, mix together the cider vinegar and ketchup.
Season with chili flakes, cayenne pepper, black pepper, and paprika.
Mix well, and store in air tight containers. This does not need to be cooked.

Chinese Steamed Buns With BBQ Pork Filling

Ingredients:

1/2 pound boneless pork loin roast | 1/2 cup barbecue sauce

3 tablespoons shallots, chopped | 1/3 cup chicken broth

1 tablespoon dark soy sauce | 1 tablespoon vegetable oil

1 tablespoon white sugar | 1 recipe Chinese Steamed Buns

Directions:

Mix together pork, barbecue sauce, shallots, flour, chicken stock, soy sauce, oil, and sugar. Chill in refrigerator for at least 6 hours.

Prepare dough for Chinese Steamed Buns.

Shape dough into balls. Roll each out into a circle, (like Won-Ton wrappers). Put 1 tablespoonful of prepared meat mixture in the center of each circle, and wrap dough around filling. Place seams down onto wax paper squares. Let stand until doubled, about 30 minutes.

Bring water to a boil in wok, and reduce heat to medium; the water should still be boiling. Place steam-plate on a small wire rack in the middle of the wok. Transfer as many buns on wax paper as will comfortably fit onto steam-plate leaving 1 to 2 inches between the buns. At least 2 inches space should be left between steam-plate and the wok. Cover wok with lid. Steam buns over boiling water for 15 to 20 minutes.

REMOVE LID BEFORE you turn off heat, or else water will drip back onto bun surface and produce yellowish "blisters" on bun surfaces. Continue steaming batches of buns until all are cooked.

Tasty BBQ
Corn on the Cob

Ingredients:

1 teaspoon chili powder

1/8 teaspoon dried oregano

1 pinch onion powder

cayenne pepper to taste

garlic powder to taste

salt and pepper to taste

1/2 cup butter, softened

6 ears corn, husked and cleaned

Directions:

Preheat grill for medium-high heat.

In a medium bowl, mix together the chili powder, oregano,
onion powder, cayenne pepper, garlic powder, salt, and pepper.
Blend in the softened butter. Apply this mixture to each ear of corn,
and place each ear onto a piece of aluminum foil big enough to wrap
the corn. Wrap like a burrito, and twist the ends to close.

Place wrapped corn on the preheated grill, and cook 20 to 30 minutes,
until tender when poked with a fork. Turn corn occasionally during cooking.

Texas BBQ Chicken

8 boneless, skinless chicken breast halves

3 tablespoons brown sugar | 1 tablespoon ground paprika

1 teaspoon salt | 1 teaspoon dry mustard

1/2 teaspoon chili powder | 1/4 cup distilled white vinegar

1/8 teaspoon cayenne pepper | 2 tablespoons Worcestershire sauce

1 1/2 cups tomato-vegetable juice cocktail

1/2 cup ketchup | 1/4 cup water | 2 cloves garlic, minced

Directions:

Preheat the oven to 350 degrees F (175 degrees C).

Place the chicken breasts in a single layer in a 9x13 inch baking dish.
In a medium bowl, mix together the brown sugar, paprika, salt,
dry mustard, chili powder, vinegar, cayenne pepper, Worcestershire sauce,
vegetable juice cocktail, ketchup, water and garlic. Pour the sauce evenly
over the chicken breasts.

Bake uncovered, for 35 minutes in the preheated oven.
Remove chicken breasts, shred with a fork, and return to the sauce.
Bake in the oven for an additional 10 minutes so the chicken can soak
up more flavor. Serve on a bed of rice with freshly ground black pepper.

Red BBQ Slaw

Ingredients:

4 cups finely shredded cabbage

1/3 cup apple cider vinegar 1/3 cup ketchup

2 tablespoons white sugar

2 teaspoons crushed red pepper flakes, or to taste

2 dashes hot pepper sauce, or to taste

Directions:

Place the cabbage into a salad bowl. In a small bowl, whisk together
apple cider vinegar, ketchup, sugar, red pepper flakes,
and hot sauce until the sugar has dissolved. Pour the dressing over
the cabbage, toss thoroughly, and refrigerate at least 1 hour before serving.

Scott's Savory BBQ Sauce

Ingredients:

1 quart apple cider vinegar

1 (20 ounce) bottle ketchup

1/4 cup paprika

1 pound dark brown sugar

1/4 cup salt

1 tablespoon black pepper

2 tablespoons red pepper flakes

1 tablespoon garlic powder

1/4 cup Worcestershire sauce

1/2 cup lemon juice

Directions:

In a large container, mix together the apple cider vinegar, ketchup, paprika, brown sugar, salt, pepper, red pepper flakes, garlic powder, Worcestershire sauce and lemon juice. Pour into an empty vinegar bottle, ketchup bottle or other container and store in the refrigerator for up to 1 month.

My Dad's BBQ Sauce

Ingredients:

2 cups barbeque sauce | 2 cups red wine

2 tablespoons onion powder | 2 tablespoons garlic powder

1/4 cup Worcestershire sauce | 2 tablespoons monosodium glutamate

1 teaspoon hot pepper sauce

Directions:

In a medium bowl, thoroughly mix the barbeque sauce, wine,
onion powder, garlic powder, Worcestershire sauce, meat tenderizer and
hot pepper sauce.

107

Tangy BBQ Rub

Ingredients:

1/2 cup instant orange drink mix | 1 teaspoon cayenne pepper

1/2 teaspoon paprika | 1 teaspoon garlic powder

1/2 teaspoon ground allspice | 1/2 teaspoon onion salt

Directions:

Mix together the instant orange drink mix, cayenne pepper, paprika,
garlic powder, allspice, and onion salt.
Store at room temperature in an airtight container until used.
Rub into chicken or pork and grill as desired.

CPSIA information can be obtained
at www.ICGtesting.com
Printed in the USA
BVHW090722180621
609825BV00004B/381